Laughing

Cheryl **Caldwell**

KPT PUBLISHING

They say that laughter
is good for the soul.

A baby's laughter is the most beautiful thing you'll ever hear. Unless it's 3 am, you're home alone, and you don't have a baby.

I think it's true.

Nothing makes
the heart happier.

I love you this...

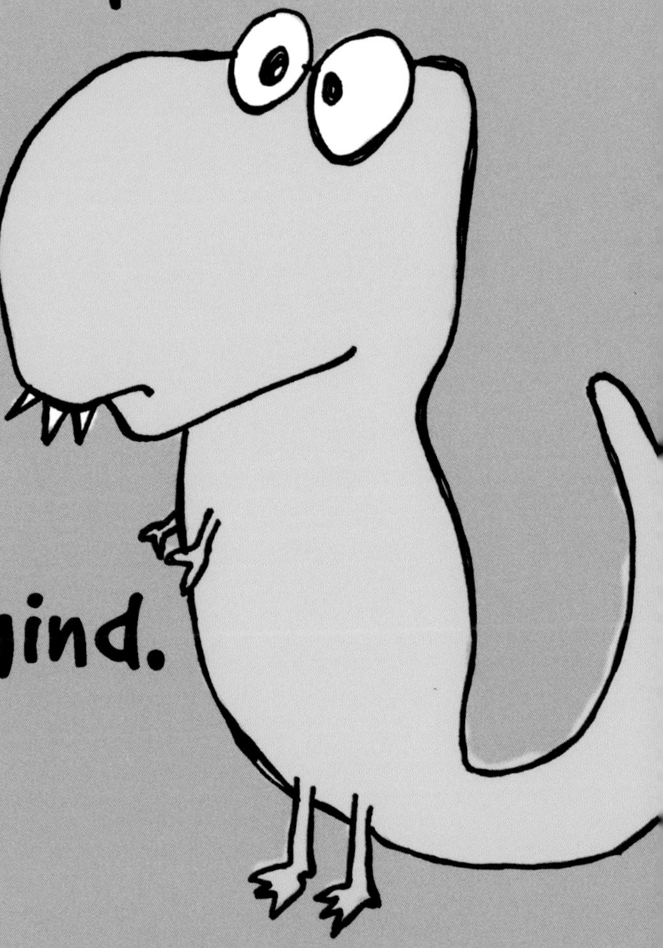

nevermind.

In fact, it's been called
the music of the heart,

My music taste ranges from "You have to hear this!" to

"Don't judge me"

the light of the soul,

When I see a light flickering,
I think:
1% electrical
problem,
99% demons.

and the best form of therapy.

I don't need "Anger Management" classes...
You need "Shut-the-hell-up" classes.

Sometimes it's
the big things...

and sometimes
it's the little things...

Not a creature was stirring...

Ralph never was one to follow the rules.

that keep us laughing.

I'm the type person who will bust out laughing in the middle of dead silence because of something that happened yesterday.

We laugh at others.

In my whole life, I've never seen anyone fall because of a banana.

We laugh at ourselves.

But the best of times
are when we laugh together.

When one goes out, they all go out.

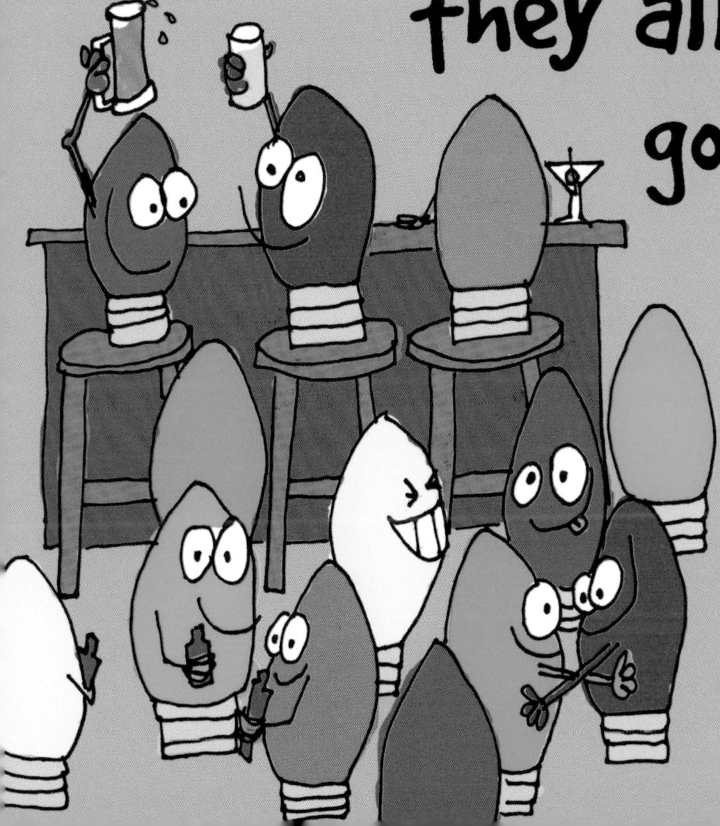

We don't all have
the same sense of humor,

but it's certainly helpful
to have one.

Laughter helps us through the rough times.

Better days are coming. They're called Saturday and Sunday.

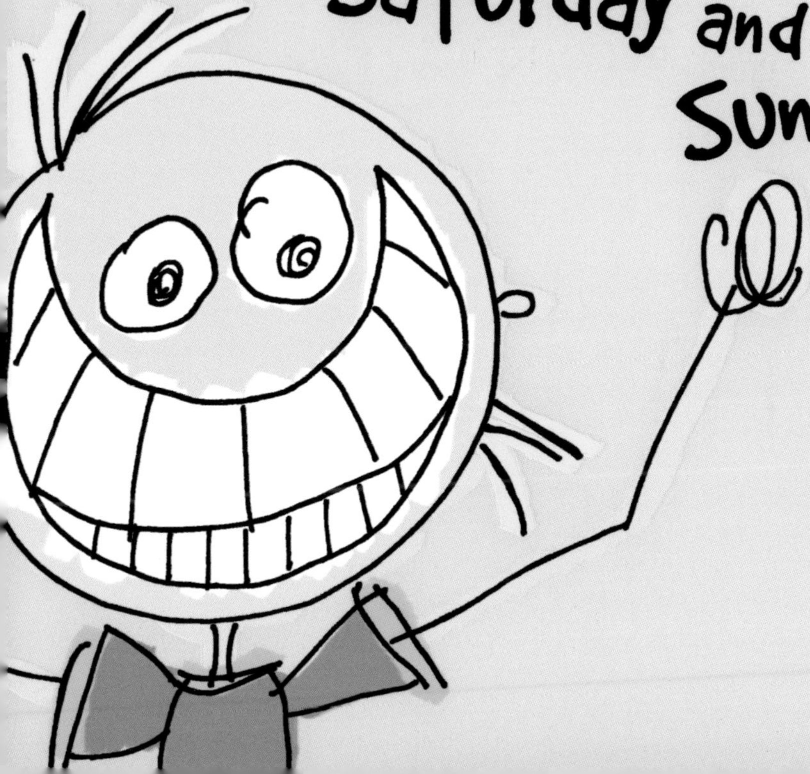

and makes the good times
that much better.

We all have that funny friend...

and the ones who *think* they are funny.

I was about to tell them to quit acting stupid.

Then I realized they weren't acting.

There are inside jokes

and jokes for the masses.

Laughter is contagious.

I'm not laughing at you. I'm laughing with you. You just aren't joining in.

Especially when you
are supposed to be serious.

Someday we will look back on this and laugh... (nervously and then quickly change the subject)!

Because life is simply better
when you are laughing.

I love it when somebody's laugh is even funnier than the joke.

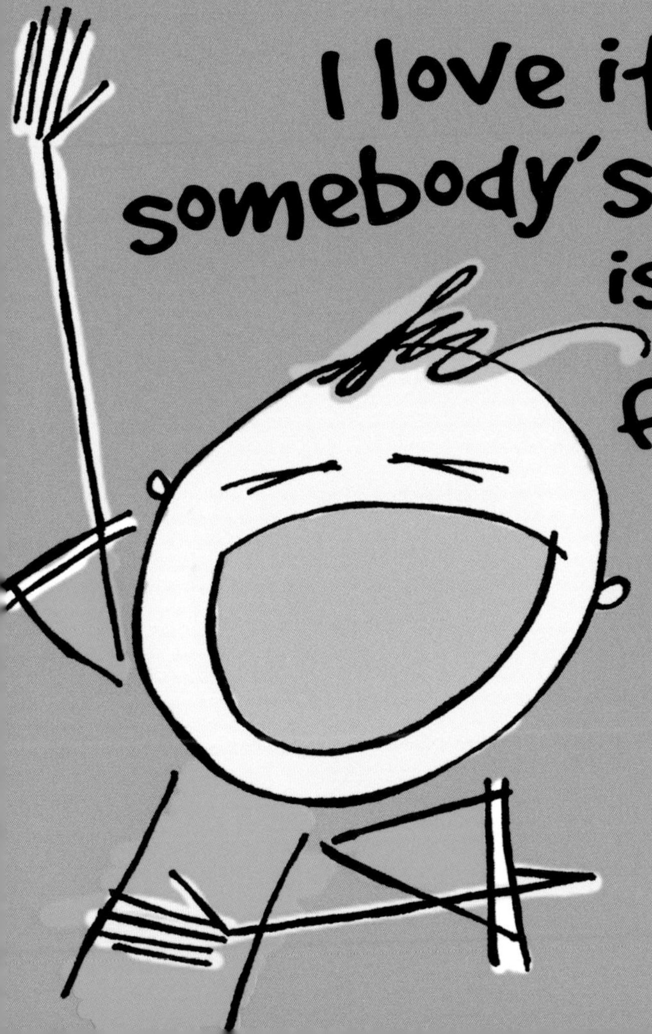

About the Author

Cheryl **Caldwell** is a sometimes artist, photographer, filmmaker, marine aquarist, and author. Most of her inspiration comes from her unconventional view of the world and the fact that she finds the mundane hilarious. She is owner of Co-edikit®, a humor based company that pairs comical illustrations with a witty combination of clear cut, down-to-earth words of wisdom and sarcastic humor. Her artwork and characters have been licensed and sold throughout the world. Her original paintings of the Co-edikit® characters can be found in several art galleries in the U.S., including Bee Galleries in New Orleans. She still subscribes to the philosophy that if you're having a bad day, ask a four- or five-year-old to skip. It's hysterical.

Laughing

Copyright © 2017 Cheryl Caldwell

Published by KPT Publishing
Minneapolis, Minnesota 55406
www.KPTPublishing.com

ISBN: 978-1-944833-23-7

Design and production by Koechel Peterson and Associates, Minneapolis, Minnesota

First printing March 2017

10 9 8 7 6 5 4 3 2 1

Printed in the United States of America